School Projects

SURVIVAL GUIDES

Writing Reports

Barbara A. Somervill

www.heinemann.co.uk/library
Visit our website to find out more information about Heinemann Library books.

To order:
☎ Phone 44 (0) 1865 888066
🖹 Send a fax to 44 (0) 1865 314091
💻 Visit the Heinemann bookshop at www.heinemann.co.uk/library to browse our catalogue and order online.

Heinemann Library is an imprint of Pearson Education Limited, a company incorporated in England and Wales having its registered office at Edinburgh Gate, Harlow, Essex, CM20 2JE – Registered company number: 00872828

"Heinemann" is a registered trademark of Pearson Education Limited

Edited by Nancy Dickmann and Kate DeVilliers
Designed by Richard Parker and Hart McLeod
Picture research by Mica Brancic
Production by Victoria Fitzgerald

Originated by Dot Gradations Ltd
Printed in China by Leo Paper Group

ISBN 978 0 431931 77 7
13 12 11 10 09
10 9 8 7 6 5 4 3 2 1

British Library Cataloguing in Publication Data
Somervill, Barbara A.
    Writing reports. – (School projects survival guides)
    371.3'0281

A full catalogue record for this book is available from the British Library.

Acknowledgements
We would like to thank the following for permission to reproduce photographs: ©Corbis pp. 12 (Brand X), 16 (Frank Trapper), 24 (zefa/Gregor Schuster); © Getty Images pp. 8 (Photodisc), 27 (Digital Vision).

Note paper design features with permission of ©istockphoto.com.

Every effort has been made to contact copyright holders of material reproduced in this book. Any omissions will be rectified in subsequent printings if notice is given to the publishers.

Contents

What is a written report? 4

Choosing a topic 8

Diving into research 10

Taking notes and organizing 14

Writing the rough draft 18

Editing and revising 22

Publishing the report 24

Planning tools 28

Research resources 30

Glossary 31

Index 32

Some words are printed in bold, **like this**. You can find out what they mean by looking in the glossary.

What is a written report?

Report planner

Step 1: Write down the project and its requirements.

Step 2: Record the due date.

Step 3: Get started immediately!

"We can learn a great deal from ancient **cultures**," says the teacher. "Today, we are going to begin working on a written report. You will choose an ancient culture to study." Matt writes down the project. The report must have at least three pages of written material and one illustration.

Understand the project

Do you worry about doing a long writing project? You can make any writing project manageable by breaking it up into small parts. A long report is just a series of paragraphs linked together. If you can write a paragraph, you can produce a written report. You need to do enough **research** and plan enough writing time to create the required amount of writing.

What is the subject area? How long does the report need to be? What support material can be used? How much time do you have to do the work? These are questions your teacher will answer when giving the project. If you have other questions, make sure you ask them. Then it is time to make a schedule. Spread out the different tasks involved in writing a report by doing at least part of one job every day.

Written reports

Written reports do several jobs. In some way, all written reports provide information. The report can also offer a **demonstration**, as often happens in a science report. Written material can **persuade** and it can also entertain the reader.

A written report about ancient Egypt will provide the reader with information. Written material used to **demonstrate** tells the reader how something is built or works. The author might demonstrate how a pyramid is built with a diagram. Persuasive writing influences a reader to think in a certain way. Writing that interests readers, particularly stories, may be entertaining.

Types of written reports

Type of report	Possible elements to include	Possible visual aids
Biography	• Birth and death dates • Major accomplishments • Primary source material	• Timeline • Portrait • Picture connected to life events
Book report	• Author and title • Characters • Setting • Plot	• Illustration • Fictional map
Science report	• Explanation of a process • List of materials • Experiments • Results	• Diagram • Chart • Graph • Illustration
Geography/history	• Cause and effect • Problem and solution • Famous people involved • Reason for importance	• Timeline • Illustration • Map of the region

Make a schedule

To make sure you get your work done on time, begin by setting up a schedule that includes all of the different parts of your project. Start your project early enough to allow plenty of time to get everything finished.

Many different tasks make up a written report. You will need to choose a topic and do research about the subject. You will need to take notes and organize your ideas. Only then can you begin to write your report.

Make a schedule that allows you to get the work done on time. Here is an example:

	Monday	Tuesday	Wednesday	Thursday	Friday
First week	1 Make a schedule	2 Choose a topic	3 Research	4 Research	5 Research
Second week	8 Research	9 Sort information	10 Make an outline	11 Begin writing	12 Write
Third week	15 Write	16 Create visual aids	17 Edit wrtiting	18 Produce a final copy	19 Hand in report

Parts of the report

Every written report must have three sections: an **introduction**, a **body**, and a **conclusion**. Written reports may also use features seen in school textbooks. Each major section may be separated by a **heading**. You might add visual aids, and those aids should have captions. At the end of the report, you will need to provide a list of the **reference** materials you used.

An introduction has two jobs. First, it must tell the reader what the topic is. Second, it must catch the reader's attention. A good introduction should not take up more than two paragraphs.

The body presents the main ideas about the topic and supporting facts or details. As you write the body, make sure you stick to the subject of the report. Each paragraph should have a topic sentence and at least two or three supporting facts. Organize your material in a clear order, such as by time or **sequence**. Then, connect your paragraphs using linking words or phrases, called **transitions**.

The body provides the main ideas and facts or details that support the main ideas. The body makes up the bulk of the report. In a three-page report, for instance, the body should take up about two pages. The introduction and conclusion take up no more than half a page each. You might need to add visual aids, such as charts, graphs, maps, or illustrations. If so, the visual aids are not included in the three pages you must write.

The conclusion, like the introduction, is short. You will want to conclude the subject and leave the reader with something to think about. You might choose to repeat two or three key ideas presented in the body. Use only one or two paragraphs for a solid conclusion.

CHAPTER CHECKLIST

✓ I understand what the assignment requires.
✓ I made a schedule.
✓ I know the parts of a report.

Choosing a topic

Report planner

Step 1: Consider possible subjects.

Step 2: Do pre-research.

Step 3: Choose one subject.

Matt must decide which ancient culture to research. He is interested in ancient Egypt, but the topic may be too large for a short written report. Matt does some **pre-research**. He goes online and does a search for "ancient Egypt". There is too much information available, so Matt narrows his topic to pyramids.

Choosing the right topic

The right topic for your report is one that appeals to you. Researching and writing a report is a learning experience. You want to choose a topic that is interesting, fun, and challenging. The more interest you have in your subject, the better your writing will be. Your teacher may assign topics in the class. If that happens, begin by looking for interesting information about your subject. This way, you can create your own excitement.

Do some pre-research to find out if there is enough available material on your topic. Look up the subject on an Internet **search engine** or use **OPAC** in the library. If there is plenty of material available, your research will be easier.

If your topic is too broad, look for a sub-topic that will be easier to research, such as Egyptian pyramids.

Expanding or narrowing a topic

A topic can be too large or too small to make a good report subject. You cannot cover the entire Roman Empire in three or four pages. Some authors have written more than 1,000 pages on the Romans and still not covered every detail. A better choice might be to narrow the topic to how everyday Romans lived.

There are many ways to expand or narrow a topic. Think about the topic from different angles. There are many ancient cultures to study, including the Aztec, ancient Greek, and Mayan cultures. One angle of approach might be studying just the Maya. Another idea might be to study ancient art in Central America. A third idea might be the Mayan calendar. As you narrow your topic, make sure you are still meeting the assignment requirements. If you are not sure, ask your teacher.

As you narrow your topic, work out its most important parts. For example, if your topic is Egyptian pyramids, think about how they were built. Who designed the pyramids? What was a pyramid like inside? Outside? What was their purpose? What interesting facts can you find out about pyramids? As you begin your research, find answers to each of your questions.

Narrow your topic to a reasonable size.

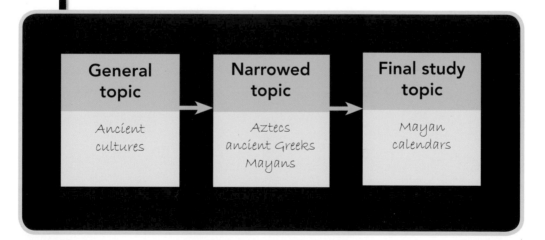

General topic	Narrowed topic	Final study topic
Ancient cultures	Aztecs ancient Greeks Mayans	Mayan calendars

CHAPTER CHECKLIST

✓ I considered possible topics.
✓ I did research to narrow my choices.
✓ I chose a specific topic.

Diving into research

Report planner

Step 1: Visit the library.

Step 2: Search the Internet.

Step 3: Find primary sources.

Matt begins his research by filling in a **planning tool** known as a KWL chart. KWL stands for "what you Know, what you Want to know, and what you have Learned". He already knows a few things about Egyptian rulers and pyramids. He records what he wants to know. These topics are the main ideas Matt will write about in his report. Matt goes to the library and asks the librarian for help. She finds several books that will help him, as well as a magazine article and a DVD on Matt's topic.

In the library

Libraries are organized to make finding information easy. Most public libraries have adult and children's sections. Libraries sort materials by fiction and non-fiction. Non-fiction materials include books, videos, audio books, magazines, newspapers, and other reference material.

Use a KWL chart to begin your research.

What you KNOW	What you WANT to know	What you have LEARNED
• Egyptians built pyramids • They were tombs • Only pharaohs and their queens had pyramids	• What do they look like inside? • Why were they so large? • When were they built? • Who did the building? • How were they built?	?

Begin your research by searching OPAC. You can search by title, author, or subject. OPAC lists books, videos, DVDs, and audiotapes. These are called sources. You should use several different sources to get your information. Collect at least three to five books, magazine articles, or videos to find the material you need.

The non-fiction section is organized according to the **Dewey decimal system**. Every non-fiction subject has an assigned number. For example, you will find Vikings listed under 948.022. When you find the catalog number for your subject, look in both the adult and children's sections. You should be able to use many adult books in your research.

HELPFUL HINT!

Collect more material than you need. To write a three-page article, many professional writers may read 30 or more pages of research. The more you know about a topic, the easier it is to write your report.

The table of contents and index

In doing research on Victorian Britain, you might find a dozen books on the subject. Take a research shortcut. Scan the table of contents and the index. Not all of these books have the material you need. Scan the table of contents in the front of the book, looking for a chapter on the lives of children, factory work, or Charles Dickens (an author who wrote about the difficult lives many children had). Also, look in the index in the back of the book to see if there are specific pages on which children are mentioned. These shortcuts can quickly determine if a book has the information you need.

Using a search engine

Many people do research on the Internet, and there is plenty of material available. The best way to find what you need is to use a search engine. A search engine finds articles and websites on a specific topic in seconds.

Control your search by defining the narrowest possible topic. You are looking for material on Victorian children. In the search window, enter "Victorian children". Those three words will narrow your search and find articles and websites you can use. Before clicking on a site address, read the description of the material offered. In this way you can quickly find the particular information you want.

Some websites will also have lists of links to other websites on similar topics. Keep a note pad by the computer. You can write down or bookmark the addresses of the best sites you find. That way, you can easily return to those sites again.

Librarians can find excellent material for any project you work on. Ask them for help!

.edu, .gov, .org

When a search list pops up, you must sort accurate sources from those that are not as reliable. On the Internet, it is best to look for sources that have .gov, .org, or .edu at the end of their addresses. Government agencies run .gov websites. Org refers to organizations, such as zoos, museums, charities, or conservation groups. Edu is the address for schools, colleges, and universities. Websites and articles with these addresses usually provide accurate information. Businesses and individuals run websites with .com addresses. They may or may not have accurate information.

Primary sources

Primary source material includes eyewitness reports and can take many forms. Typical primary sources might include diaries, letters, court or government records, interviews, or videos. An example of a primary source that can be used for researching pyramids would be **hieroglyphics** from a pyramid wall. Secondary sources describe, report, or explain information. A secondary source would be a description of how the hieroglyphics were translated.

People who are experts in the subject of your report are excellent sources. Experts on ancient cultures may be found at museums, colleges, or universities. You might find their names in magazine articles or in a television interview. Usually, the expert is introduced by name and where they work. Look up the workplace on the Internet, find the address, and send a note or email with your questions. You'll be surprised by how many experts and organizations will help students.

CHAPTER CHECKLIST

✓ I made a list of information I needed.
✓ I found that information at the library or on the Internet.
✓ I found a primary source to use in my report.

Taking notes and organizing

Report planner

Step 1: Take careful notes.

Step 2: Put the notes in logical order.

Step 3: Use a planning tool or outline.

Matt collects plenty of material on pyramids and begins taking notes. He decides to use a note **grid** to help sort all the information he has. He tapes several sheets of lined paper together and makes a large grid. He will enter all of his notes onto the grid.

Take notes

When you do research for a big project, take your notes using a note grid or index cards. To make a note grid, tape together several sheets of paper to form a large rectangle. You should draw lines on the page to make a grid. Allow room to write four or five sentences in each grid block. Along the top, write "Resources" followed by notes.

WRITE LIKE A PRO!

Plagiarism – don't do it! Plagiarism is copying another author's writing word-for-word. This is against the law. You may use short quotes as long as you give the author credit for the material. If you are not using a quote, just read the material and take notes of the important facts in your own words.

Write the resource information, including the author, title, publisher, place of publication, and date of publication in boxes along the left-hand side. All notes in that row will come from that source. When you take notes from a new resource, begin a new row. For quotes, write the entire quote word-for-word in the appropriate box. Be sure to add the page number where you found the quote.

Index cards come in several sizes. On the top of each card, write the subject of the note, the source, and the page number where the information was found. Then, write the information you found in your own words. This will help for sorting notes later on.

 Make a note grid to help organize your research. Here is an example:

Topic: Ancient pyramids Resources	Types of pyramids	Pyramid shape
"Pyramids: House of Eternity" British Museum, www.ancientegypt.co.uk/ pyramids/home.html	• earliest royal burials, dug pits, covered with mound of earth • Djoser, built at Saqqara, looks like multi-layered wedding cake • Giza, fourth dynasty, built with large stones, pyramid of Cheops, what we think of as pyramids	• several ideas about shape 1. represented what land looked like when the earth was formed, based on hill shape 2. angle on sides let pharaoh climb to heaven 3. rays of sun
Reach for the Stars: Ancient Egyptian Pyramids Brian Williams Raintree, 2007	• built with slave labour • large stones carved by hand • hard to move – took many slaves to haul one block into place	• stones got smaller toward top • hallways and rooms inside • designed to protect the remains of pharaohs and their wealth

Just the facts

Whether you use a grid or note cards, each note should be short. Just write the facts, details, dates, or other important information on one topic. If you change topics, you need to use a new note card or new grid section. For example, you research ancient Egyptian lifestyles. Put information about food on one card, clothing on another, and housing on yet another. Each time you take notes from a new source, use a new card.

You might wish to include a quote from another author or an expert in your material. Quotes add power to your writing, because they support your ideas. To use another author's words you must give them credit. An example of citing an author's work would be, In *Empire of the Inca*, Somervill says, "The early history of the Incas is bound up with myths that are difficult to separate from facts."

Sorting and organizing information

Once you have taken your notes, you need to organize your ideas. Two good ways to organize your ideas are writing an outline or using a planning tool. An outline arranges material in the order in which it is to be presented. Outlines have three basic parts: main ideas, sub-topics, and supporting details. Main ideas are labelled I, II, III, and so on. Under each main idea place the sub-topics (a, b, c) and place supporting details (1, 2, 3) under each sub-topic.

Planning tools help sort large amounts of information. Different tools work well for different types of information. You do not need to use complete sentences on a planning tool. Just put the main ideas and facts down in short phrases.

Interesting facts about your chosen topic can come from a variety of sources.

You can find examples of useful planning tools at the end of this book or on the Internet. Use a planning tool to divide your ideas into smaller categories. Then, sort your notes according to those categories. Put note cards in the order in which you plan to use the information and number each card in order. You are ready to begin writing.

Make an outline before you begin writing your report. Here is an example:

Everyday life in Greece

I. Houses
  a. Furniture
  b. Construction

II. Children
  a. Education
  b. Clothing
  c. Entertainment

III. Adults
  a. Work
    1. Trade
    2. Hunting
    3. Farming
  b. Clothing
  c. Entertainment

CHAPTER CHECKLIST

✓ I took notes.
✓ I recorded my sources.
✓ I organized my materials.

Writing the rough draft

Report planner

Step 1: Write an interesting introduction.

Step 2: Arrange the body in a clear order.

Step 3: Wrap up your thoughts in a strong conclusion.

Matt has used a main idea chart to sort his facts. He has written a different chart for each main idea. Matt knows that he needs many facts to write a written report. He uses nine idea organizers, and each one stands for a paragraph in the body.

Getting the opening right

After looking through your notes, decide what information would make a good introduction for your report. You might want to start with a quote. Another good opener is a fascinating fact. Give the fact, and then draw the reader in by explaining how that fact connects to your topic. Here is an example: "Despite what appears in films, mummies are not found in Egyptian pyramids. Mummies come from tombs in the Valley of the Kings."

Use a main idea chart to sort information. Here is an example:

Main idea:	Fact:
	Estimate – 591,000 stone blocks on outside
	Fact: Built during reign of Khufu, about 2,720–2,560 BCE
The Great Pyramid at Giza	**Fact:** One of seven wonders of the world
	Fact: Two rooms, many interior shafts
	Fact: Pyramids of Giza among the oldest human-built structures still standing
	Fact: Great Pyramid – last remaining of the Seven Wonders of the Ancient World.

A third idea might be to connect your topic to something current. For example: "Recently, workers repairing the surface of Egypt's Great Sphinx found a passage into the centre. That passage lay hidden for thousands of years. What might be buried deep inside the sphinx?"

Filling out the body

Review your remaining notes and make sure they are in the order in which you plan to write the body. Now, it is time to change your notes into paragraphs. Write a topic sentence that covers the main idea. Then, produce two to four sentences that support the main idea.

Once you have written the body, look over your writing. Make sure that each paragraph has a topic sentence. See that each paragraph focuses on one main idea, and the supporting sentences provide facts about that idea.

WRITE LIKE A PRO!

Make your writing come alive by using active verbs. An active verb is one that shows some type of action, such as walk, run, write, build, eat, and sleep. Write: The Roman Empire conquered countries throughout Europe. Try not to write: Countries were conquered by the Romans.

Turn each of your main ideas into a paragraph in your written report. Here is an example:

Main idea: Inca agriculture	Notes turned into a paragraph:
• main crop – potatoes • other crops – manioc, avocados, guavas, pineapples • several hundred species of potato • freeze-drying, chuño	Agriculture played a major role in the Inca economy. The main crop was the potato, although Incas also grew manioc, guavas, avocados, and pineapples. The Incas grew several hundred different varieties of potatoes. They also developed a way to freeze-dry potatoes. Throughout the long Andes winters, Inca families ate freeze-dried potatoes, called chuño, in soups and stews.

Transitions and voice or tone

Help your writing flow by adding words and phrases that connect sentences and paragraphs. These links are called **transitions**. You wish to connect pyramid murals and mummies together. You might write something like, "A pharaoh's treasure lay in a secret room in a pyramid. In many such rooms, a mural of the pharaoh's life story decorated the chamber walls."

If you find an area where your writing seems boring, add lively words. Try to use sight, hearing, taste, smell, and touch in your writing. Include descriptions such as the sounds of an army marching or the smell of village streets.

A writer's voice or tone is the view the writer takes towards the subject. Your personality shows through in your writing. Every writer has a style, and you do too. The words you choose and how you put them together make up your style. Remember your audience as you write. Try not to use many words that are hard for your readers to understand. The best way to develop your style is to be yourself. Write much like you speak – that is your writer's voice.

A strong conclusion

A conclusion needs to be as short as an introduction. Again, three or four sentences may be enough to wrap up your ideas. The purpose of a conclusion is to summarize your main idea and leave the audience with something to think about.

Begin by restating the main idea of your report. Then, end the same way you began. Use a quote, a fascinating fact, or some connection to other information the audience already knows.

WRITE LIKE A PRO!

A thesaurus lists many synonyms that can add variety to your writing. A synonym is a word with the same or similar meaning, such as "home" and "house". Beware! Not every synonym has exactly the same meaning. *Knowledge, folklore, and folkways* are all synonyms for culture, but they cannot always replace each other. Make sure you know the full meaning of a synonym before you use it in your writing.

CHAPTER CHECKLIST

✓ I have written an interesting introduction.
✓ I included facts and details in the body.
✓ I finished the report with a strong conclusion.

Editing and revising

Report planner

Step 1: Review the goals of good writing.

Step 2: Look for spelling and grammar errors.

Step 3: Make corrections in your writing.

Matt reviews his paper for mistakes. He fixes spelling errors and a few mistakes in grammar. To make the writing more interesting, he adds lively descriptions. Matt writes a paragraph about working in the desert heat. He tells about men straining to move large stone blocks. These details make his writing more interesting to read.

The process of turning a rough **draft** into a finished report is called editing. All writers edit their work. It is editing that smoothes out rough areas, gets rid of **repetition**, and creates a better report.

HELPFUL HINT!

If you are working on a computer, print off your report for editing. Pages look different on a computer screen from the way they do on paper. You'll find editing is easier when marking a page with a pen.

Elements of good writing

Begin the editing process by seeing if you have met the goals of good writing. For example, you need to check the flow of the writing. Do the ideas in your report move in an order that makes sense? Common ways to organize ideas include by time, importance, or causes and effects. You planned your organization before you started writing. Now, you need to read and check if you have followed that pattern. For example, you wrote about the Roman Empire. In error, you placed the Emperor Caligula before Julius Caesar. Fix this problem by switching the sections. When you move material around, you should use transitions that help the reader move through the information.

The editing process

Take your time with the editing process. You are looking for small errors, such as a misplaced comma or incorrect spelling. Start your proofreading by reading line by line. You could use a ruler under each sentence. Although this might sound silly, the ruler slows down your reading and helps you find mistakes.

As you read, review every sentence for a subject and a verb. When you find a **sentence fragment**, correct it. Your sentences should vary in length, both short and long. If you have many short sentences combine two of them by using *and*, *or, but*, or *yet*. If you find sentences that seem too long, break them into two shorter sentences.

Remember to use vocabulary that the readers – and you – understand. Fancy wording does not necessarily make for good writing. The best report is one that is clearly written, easily understood, and keeps the reader interested.

Goals of good writing

Goal	Features
Building ideas	Finding new facts or details, finding quotes, doing research, presenting facts in an order that the reader can understand them
Focused writing	Follow through with one theme and provide support for that topic
Mechanics	Grammar, spelling, punctuation, correct word usage
Organization	Time order, compare and contrast ideas or events, order of importance, problems and their solutions, causes and their effects
Style	Tone of voice, lively descriptions, varying sentence lengths, use five senses

CHAPTER CHECKLIST

✓ I checked the organization of the report.
✓ I fixed errors.
✓ I used easy-to-understand words.

Publishing the report

Report planner

Step 1: Add visual aids.

Step 2: Write a reference section.

Step 3: Publish the report.

Matt follows his project schedule. After editing his report, he begins making a final copy. He uses his best handwriting to make the final copy. Matt decides to add a map of Egypt marked with the major pyramid sites. He also draws a picture similar to one found in a pyramid. By following his plan, Matt can hand in his written report on time.

Adding visual aids

Adding visual aids to your report makes the paper more interesting. Diagrams, charts, and graphs improve science, maths, and geography reports. Make sure you label the information clearly. Write a caption below the visual aid to describe what the material shows. You will want to give credit for any artwork you do not make yourself.

Egyptians decorated the walls of pyramids with pictures and hieroglyphics, which were a way of writing using pictures.

If you copy a picture or map from the Internet or a book, make sure you give credit to the source. For example, Egyptian hieroglyphs, *The Pocket Guide to Ancient Egyptian Hieroglyphs* by Richard Parkinson, page X.

The type of material you use depends on the type of report. A map, timeline, or illustration adds to a history report. A map should cover the land being discussed and some of the surroundings. A timeline should connect key dates to events the reader might already know about. For instance, a timeline about the Aztecs says, "1325, First Aztec temple is built in Tenochtitlan." You might add, "1347, The Black Death sweeps across Europe."

Computer v. handwriting

If the teacher does not ask for a typed report, you may handwrite it. Make sure you use your best handwriting. You want to produce a very neat report, not one filled with blotches and cross-outs. A handwritten report should be written on lined paper. Illustrations and the cover page, however, might be produced on plain paper.

If you can type neatly and have the time to do so, that's fine. Double-space the report to make it easier to read. Use the spell check to look for errors. Although the spell check is helpful, it does not catch every mistake. For example, a mistyped "does" may appear as "dose". If your error makes a real word, spell check will not catch it.

Read through the paper several times to find errors before you print your final copy. One way to find mistakes is to read each line of text from the bottom of the page to the top. Mistakes pop out using this technique.

The cover page

Your teacher may ask for a cover page. You should use the format your teacher asks for. Here are directions for one type of cover sheet. If you are using lined paper, write the title five lines from the top. Centre your title. You may use all capital letters or just capitalize the first word.

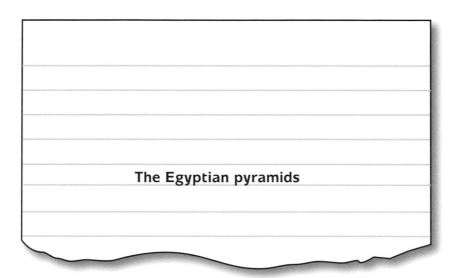

The Egyptian pyramids

About six lines from the bottom of the page, also in the centre, write your name. Under your name, write your class, and, below that, the date.

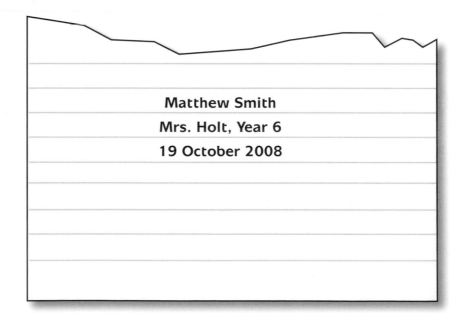

Matthew Smith

Mrs. Holt, Year 6

19 October 2008

When you hand in your report, make sure it is neat, clearly written, and readable.

A table of contents

If your report has five or more pages, you might want to put a table of contents after the cover page. If you use a table of contents, you may have to add subheads to separate each section. This book uses subheads, and the one for this section is "A table of contents". Your table of contents might include Introduction, Early pyramids, Map of Egypt, The Great Pyramid, Inside the pyramids, Egyptian writing, Conclusion, and References.

References

On a separate page, list all the references you used to get your information. If you use a quote, you must include that source in your list. You should also list books, DVDs or videos, articles, and Internet websites. You will need to list the author, title, publisher, place of publication, and date of publication. Each reference item has a specific format you will need to use. Ask your teacher what format to use for listing a reference.

What did you learn?

When you have every part of your written report complete, put it together and hand it in. Think about what you learned doing this project. You probably learned new information about your subject. You also learned how to do research and how to take notes. You worked out a way to organize the material you collected. In addition, you improved your writing. These skills will be used again, both in school and later in life. Congratulations! You have turned a simple project into a success.

CHAPTER CHECKLIST

✓ I added visual aids to my report.
✓ I put the report together neatly.
✓ I finished my report on time.

Planning tools

Planning tools help you sort research, understand study materials, and study for tests. Choose one that fits your needs.

KWL (Know-Want-Learn)

Complete the "K" section of the KWL chart by filling in the information you already know about the topic. Determine what you want to learn and note it under "W". As you do your research, add new information under the "L" section.

What you KNOW	What you WANT to know	What you have LEARNED

Main idea

Use this chart to identify the main idea of a passage or paragraph and the information that supports the main idea.

	Supporting information:
Main idea:	Supporting information:
	Supporting information:

5 Ws and 1 H

The 5 Ws and I H stand for who, what, when, where, why, and how. When writing about or studying history, this is a good chart to use.

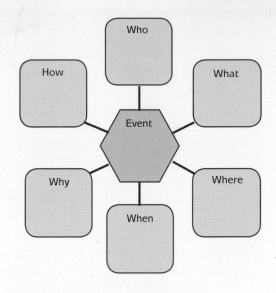

Cause and effect

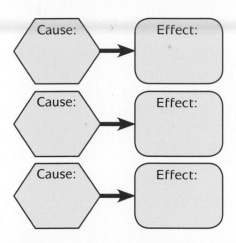

A cause-and-effect chart allows you to relate events (causes) and the results (effects) of those events. A cause-and-effect chart works well for discussing scientific processes, historical events, and how or why something happened.

Chain of events

When trying to organize a sequence of events, use a chain of events chart. It is particularly good for arranging information for a biography or history report.

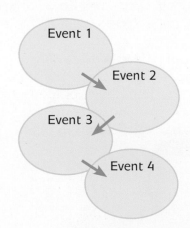

Research resources

In the library

Almanacs
An almanac is published every year. It contains facts, figures, and statistics on many different topics. Make sure you use the most recent edition to get current facts.

Atlases
An atlas is a book of maps, usually covering the entire world. Additional maps may show the oceans, ocean currents, agriculture, how land is used, and population.

Dictionaries
Most dictionaries do more than just give definitions of words. Standard dictionaries may contain **synonyms**, **antonyms**, usage, word origin, and pronunciation. There are also biographical and geographical dictionaries available.

Encyclopaedias
An encyclopaedia contains information on a wide variety of subjects. There are also narrower versions, such as an encyclopaedia of mammals, sports, plants, and so on.

School or public librarians
When doing research you should first talk to a librarian. Librarians know how to find information and how to get that information for you.

On the Internet

Homework help
There are many sites that offer help with homework. The BBC Schools site – www.bbc.co.uk/schools – has help on all the primary subjects.

Internet Public Library
The Internet Public Library (www.ipl.org) is like having a library on your computer. You can search through the site for information on geography, science, literature, history, and so on. You can read a book, a magazine, or a newspaper.

Online news
Most major newspapers, news magazines, and television stations have news websites. Many have search windows. Enter your topic and click "search".

Search engines
Search engines have many interesting names – Ask.com, Google, and Yahoo, to name a few. Each of these search engines works in the same way. Enter a topic in the search window, click, and the engine finds articles and websites that fill your request. Be patient. You may not find what you need on the first attempt.

Glossary

antonym word that means the opposite of another word

body main section of a speech or written piece

conclusion end of a speech or written piece

culture art, music, literature, beliefs, and customs of a group of people

demonstrate show how something works

demonstration display given to others to show how something is done or how something works

Dewey decimal system system of arranging non-fiction materials by assigning numbers to specific topics

draft early version of a written document

grid network of evenly spaced rectangles

heading caption printed at the top of an article or book, usually in bold letters

hieroglyphics writing system that uses symbols or pictures to represent words or ideas

introduction opening of a speech or written piece

OPAC (Online Public Access Catalogue) tool for finding library materials by author, title, or subject

persuade convince someone

plagiarism using someone else's written ideas without giving them credit for the material

planning tool visual aid for sorting information

pre-research looking into a topic before beginning the actual project

primary source document or film in which a person relates an eyewitness view of an event

reference source of information

repetition process of saying or writing something again

research look up information about a subject

search engine program on the Internet designed to find articles and websites on specific topics

sentence fragment incomplete sentence, missing either the subject or verb

sequence group of items arranged in a particular order

synonym word with the same or similar meaning, such as "home" and "house"

transition word or phrase linking two ideas

Index

body 6, 7, 18, 19

caption(s) 6, 24
chart(s) 5, 7, 24, 29
conclusion 6, 7, 18, 20
cover page 25, 26, 27

details 6, 7, 16, 23
Dewey decimal system 11
diagram(s) 5, 24

editing 7, 22, 23, 24

facts 6, 7, 9, 16, 18, 19, 20, 23
fiction 10

grammar 22, 23
graph(s) 5, 7, 24
grid 14, 16

heading 6

illustration(s) 4, 5, 7, 25
index 11
index cards 14, 15
Internet 12, 13, 25, 27
introduction 6, 7, 20, 27

library 8, 10

main idea(s) 6, 7, 10, 16, 18, 19,
    20, 21, 28
map(s) 5, 7, 25, 27

non-fiction 10, 11
notes 6, 14, 15, 16, 18, 19, 27

OPAC 8, 11
outline 7, 16, 17

paragraph(s) 4, 7, 18, 19, 20, 21, 22
persuasive writing 5
plagiarism 17
planning tool(s) 10, 14, 16, 17, 28
pre-research 8
primary source 13
proofreading 23

quote(s) 15, 16, 17, 18, 20, 23, 27

reference(s) 6, 10, 27
research 4, 6, 8, 9, 10, 11, 12, 14,
    16, 23, 27, 28
revising 22
rough draft 22

search engine(s) 12, 30
secondary source 13
schedule 4, 6, 7
sequence 6
source(s) 11, 13, 15, 27
spelling 22, 23
style 20
sub-topic(s) 8, 16
synonym(s) 21, 30

table of contents 11, 27
thesaurus 21
timeline 5, 23
tone 20, 23
topic(s) 6, 8, 10, 18, 23
topic sentence 19
transition(s) 6, 20, 22

visual aids 5, 6, 7, 24, 27
voice 20

website(s) 12, 13